# ILLEGITIMAC

C000245013

## Introduction

Every child has a father and mother. If the couple are not married at the time of the birth, then the child is illegitimate. There is nothing new, unusual or shocking about illegitimacy - there is a lot of it about, there always has been and probably always will be. Sooner or later, most family historians come across it among their own ancestors, unless they were very under-sexed or more cunning than average at concealment. In most cases, it is no bar to further search, since the father's name can be discovered and the hunt proceed as normal.

## Some bastards are more equal than others

There always used to be a distinction in the public attitude to different sorts of bastards, according to their provenance. In descending order of acceptance:-

1. The child of a couple who intend to marry when possible (or where the man died before the wedding or deserted at the last moment).
2. The child of a stable relationship where the couple cannot (or will not) marry for a valid reason (mad wife, deserting husband, religious scruples).
3. The children of a rich man's mistress.
4. The product of casual seduction of a young girl.
5. The children of a poor man's steady mistress.
6. The children of a prostitute or promiscuous amateur.
7. The child of a married woman by another man.
8. The child of incest.

Although there was almost always a financial disadvantage (except for class 3) there was rarely much social stigma which mattered, except in the upper and middle classes. The Parson was paid to moralise and sometimes did. The Squire's spinster sister might sneer at a temptation which had never come her way, but for most ordinary folk, "there but for the Grace of God go I". Attitudes hardened further up the social scale as did the handicaps, but the main blame lay in not covering up in some acceptable way. In Victorian times, this passion for concealment spread down the social scale, and it is then that illegitimacy became shameful, not to be spoken about in polite society. Even the most Victorian of maiden aunts, however, relaxes if it is suggested that the father of the child was rich, a gentleman or preferably Royal, whatever the character of the man or the association.

There has always been a double standard of morality – women are expected to behave better than men, even by the men who spend their time undermining this. Therefore, any blame going has always attached to the mother rather than the illegitimate father, and it was necessary to prove to local satisfaction that she was seduced, not a tart or even a willing party. This was obviously easier in the home village, where the facts were known, than in a town. The girl who ran away from home to follow a soldier might start in class 1 to 4, but inevitably ended in class 6. The village bad girl, however, was regarded as worse than the town tart, since she was a direct threat to stable families. Even if she confined her attention to only one married man, the wives' trade union united against her and their children bullied hers. She couldn't win even if she stuck to bachelors, since they were some mothers' sons and might be forced to marry her some day.

The product of an incestuous relationship within a close family unit was treated as a leper and generally died mysteriously as an infant. There were marginal cases of incest, where the parties came within the "prohibited degrees" listed in the prayer book, and could not marry because they were related. If a man married again in old age, his grandchildren of the first marriage and children of the last were much of an age, and illegal relationships sometimes grew up between half-uncle and niece, thrown together.

And as man and wife were one flesh, their kin occupied the same technical relationship to each other, without blood ties. If a wife died, her sister might come to help out with the children, but the widower could never marry her legally, though sometimes couples went through a ceremony where they were not known. Marriage with Deceased Wife's Sister, after being an issue throughout the nineteenth century, became legal, and retrospectively so, in 1908, and the children were legitimated. This accounts for many a family feud which no one will explain, for the first family regarded the second as incestuous. In certain cases, a mother would conceal the fact that her daughter's child was incestuous, to avoid the scandal, though inevitably it soured family relationships and the child, if it lived, might be "picked on" and frightened into imbecility.

The child of a married woman is assumed to be that of her husband if they are living together, even technically.  Only if he could prove long absence, for eleven months or so, or medical incapability, could a husband have this legal presumption altered. Even the king who went down in history as Enrique el Impotente jibbed at this.   Unless it was such a public scandal that the parson recorded the true name of the father in the parish register, it is very difficult to discover true parentage.   Very many husbands may have a vague suspicion, which the appearance of the child might tend to confirm, but few would publicise their thoughts. Family tradition may hint, but truth may be almost impossible to prove.

## Pre-Victorian background

In the upper classes, the unmarried daughters and sisters represented valuable counters in the game of financial, political or territorial advancement, so they were guarded closely until such time as they could be auctioned off to the highest bidder.   It was vital to have a clearly legitimate heir to a title or landed estates, so the girl must be kept a virgin till marriage, with the aid of chaperones to be with her at all times.   If a girl of this class somehow evaded Papa's surveillance and became pregnant, she would be thrown out, hastily married off "beneath her" if the man was halfway suitable, or, in the eighteenth century, perhaps packed off to France with a mystery illness which lasted exactly nine months.  The infant would be fostered out to a lower class couple, with expenses paid and possibly some provision when the child was 14.   The arrangements were normally conducted through a friend or lawyer, and only rarely was it possible for a child to find out the truth, unless the mother blew her own cover, through idle curiosity or pangs of conscience. The exceptional bright or pretty child was sometimes taken into the natural family as "ward" or "nephew".

Below this level, there might be some manipulation by a farmer to limit the range of his daughter's acquaintance – as there is today – to other farmers' sons, but once she had selected a suitable young man, restrictions were lifted.  The betrothed couple enjoyed most of the privileges of the married couple, and if the girl became pregnant, they might accelerate the wedding, or might not, if they were busy with the harvest.  As long as the bride made it up the church steps before she went into labour, all was well.  If she became involved with an unsuitable young man, Father might refuse his consent or make the best of it and allow the marriage, or support the girl and her child till someone better came along.  One illegitimate child was neither here nor there, especially for a girl with a dowry.

Among ordinary labourers, the illegitimacy rate was inevitably higher, since even a couple who wished to marry there and then might not be able to.   The relationship remained, and they mostly married later, before the second, or maybe the third, child was due. A young male labourer often lived in at the farmhouse, and neither there nor in the over-crowded family cottage was there room for a wife and child. It was simple common sense for a local girl to stay unmarried, rather than wed an incomer with no settlement in the village (see *Other Parish Records*, page 6) and risk being thrown out with him and the baby, if he lost his job or health.

Casual sex occurred commonly between young people at "maying" time, when young people spent the night in the woods and came home covered in may blossom and blushes.  Also at harvest and Christmas, when the farmers gave feasts and alcohol loosened inhibitions; and during haying, when the climate was agreeable and the piles of hay to hand and a lot of temporary labourers were around.  If a local couple were involved they might marry and make the best of it - even a reasonable success.  But no one expected a local girl to wed some roving Welsh or Irish labourer just to "give the baby a name", when it would have her perfectly good local name.

Similarly, no one seriously expected the couple to marry if their social class was very unequal.  If the Squire's son, or a rich farmer's, got a girl in the family way, he had to pay up, not marry the girl.  Often, the pay off gave a poor girl a dowry which facilitated her marriage to the poor man she preferred anyway - which is why the blame was sometimes put on the man who could afford it, rather than the real father.  On the whole, stepfathers seem to have accepted a genuine child of a rich man, cheerfully enough, as a present financial asset and a possible future lever against landlord or employer.

## Official attitudes

The clergy had a professional duty to reprimand "incontinency" among their flock, but most of them were close enough in background to the farming community they served to accept what was natural, and they reserved their criticism for the prostitute, or for rape and incest.  Strictly, a couple who produced a bastard child had to do penance in a white sheet in the church porch (in extreme cases in the market place).  The churchwardens had a duty to "present" cases of immorality before the Bishop's apparitor, when that official made his annual rounds.  The presentments are recorded in the Bishop's registers and sometimes on the foot of the parchment containing the Bishop's transcript of the parish registers.  The custom bore most heavily on dissenters and others unpopular with the establishment.

There were more compelling reasons for taking an interest in the parentage of a bastard than moral ones.  Each parish had to care for its own poor, which normally included the unmarried mother and her child, so it required to know all about the case, with details of the father's name and origins, with the intention of claiming back some of the expenditure from him.  The parish records are the first place to look for the parentage of bastards.

## Parish registers

There are numerous ways of expressing illegitimacy:-
*Latin:* ignotus = unknown (father).
  spurius = spurious, occasionally with the father's name alone given.
  filius populi = son of the people; appears to cover cases where
    the father is local, but might be one of two.
  filius nullius = son of none; seems to cover cases where the father
    was a stranger or the girl can't or won't say.
*English:* base, bastard, spurious, supposed, imputed, misbegotten,
  chance begotten.
  "Baptised John son of Mary Brown and the reputed son of John Smith"
    means he admits it, or it has been proved.
  "Baptised John ......, the imputed son of John Smith" means she
    says so, but he won't admit it, or the case is not settled yet.
A common way of showing paternity is to give the male child his
father's full name and the girl his surname.  The idea is that if
the couple marry later, the mother's surname can be dropped.

John Smith son of Mary Brown and John Smith is legally known as
John Smith Brown until the wedding, and maybe after, if it is much
delayed.  An apparent double-barrelled name is therefore suspect, if
it occurs anywhere but in a recognised gentry family before about
1840.  In London, Lancashire, Yorkshire and among nonconformists,
the use of a complimentary second surname, from the mother's family,
the pastor, or a rich uncle, came in in the early parts of the 1800s,
and generally later in the Victorian period, until it was commonplace, very useful to genealogists, but before this, or outside the
named areas, check for illegitimacy.

An earlier example of a genuine double surname might arise where
a gentry family inherited the name of an old aristocratic family
through their heiresses, sometimes compounded, as in Twisleton-
Wykeham-Fiennes. This is very rare. Late in the nineteenth century,
people with very common names sometimes invented a similar hyphenated
surname for themselves (Armstrong-Jones, or Heygate-Browne).  This
shows snobbery (or pride in ancestry), not illegitimacy.

The printed forms in use for registers after 1813 left no real
room for entering an illegitimate father's name.  Some of the clergy
gave up, but some manged, nonetheless.

| Date  | Name of child | Name of parents | Occupation |
|-------|---------------|-----------------|------------|
| Jan 5 | John Brown    | Jane Smith      | base       |
| Jan 5 | John Brown    | Jane Smith      | spinster   |
|       |               | & John Brown    | labourer   |
| Jan 5 | John          | Jane Smith      | servant    |
|       |               | and John Brown, labourer, base child | |
| Jan 5 | John          | John Brown      | labourer   |
|       |               | & Jane Smith    |            |

The last entry leaves it in doubt - are they married?  Is the man's
name John Brown Smith, an earlier bastard perhaps?  Check the marriage registers and later baptisms for the same couple, or earlier
baptisms to see if John Brown Smith exists.

After 1837, it becomes increasingly rare for the actual registers to record the father's name at all, in deference to growing prudery. It is always worth looking at marriage registers, though, since many bastards were told who their father was at that point, and quoted it to the parson. Occasionally, a legitimate brother or sister would come along as a witness - rarely, even the father, if he lived locally. One very good reason for telling the child his name was that otherwise, the bastard might fall in love with a half-sister, legitimate or illegitimate.

## Other parish records

If the register entry says merely
"Baptised John son of Mary Brown a baseborn child"
then other sources must be tried.    Documents which would have been in the parish chest come first.

Each parish was responsible for its own poor, so when it looked probable that some village girl was expecting a baby, they made enquiries. Unmarried mothers had few possibilities of supporting themselves unless they were kept by a rich man or became prostitutes, which was profitable but short-lived, and ruined any chance of marriage later.    Therefore they mostly became chargeable on the parish.

A bastard was the responsibility of the local parish where it was born, so the sharper parishes tended to throw out any girl who looked pregnant. Later, they agreed to retain one who was their own settled inhabitant, but sent strangers back to their own parishes of settlement, encouraged by a whip if necessary.    The girl had to admit who the father was.    Mostly this would be known anyway in a village, unless it was a one night stand.    She could even be sent to prison if she refused to tell.

The young man was then sent for and shown the girl's Examination, which named him.    He was also questioned, to see if he admitted paternity on the spot.    He could:-

a. Pay the girl enough privately to keep her and the child (which he could do before it came to the Overseers' attention, and so keep his name out of it).

b. He could pay the Overseers a minimum of £40 down, representing £2 for the lying in and a shilling a week for 14 years, plus a sum to ensure that the only mention might be in the Overseers' Accounts:-
   "From John Smith about the lying in of Mary Brown".
   A persuasive man might even keep his name out of the parish registers, though most clergy did insist on showing it, if only for the sake of avoiding future incest.

c. Admit paternity and sign a Bastardy Bond, which promised to pay the lying-in expenses and maintenance at some date in the future, hoping the child would die young.    If it died within three weeks of birth, the Bond was rescinded.

d. Admit nothing or deny it all. The Overseers might talk him round, take him before the local magistrate, bring witnesses, set the

girl's brothers on him or otherwise pressure him.  He might then
agree to marry the girl, with perhaps a few shillings as a sweet-
ener from the parish, but if he still refused to sign, he would
be committed to the Assizes.

**e.** Refuse to admit it and abscond. The parish would try to track him
down, and there were a number of forms to cover this process, plus
details of expenditure in the Accounts. If brought back, the next
stage would be to pressure locally and then the Assizes.

**f.** Be brought to trial at the Assizes. It took a very determined man,
with a great many witnesses to prove he was elsewhere at the time
involved, to escape conviction. If he had been seen with the girl
at around the right time, that was it. There were no blood tests.

The first record will show the complaint:-

"Henry Barret and James Linford, Overseers of the Poor of the
parish of Slowly, against John Smith. They allege that Mary Brown
an inhabitant thereof is with child and the the child is likely
to be born a bastard and that she doth swear the aforesaid John
Smith is the father thereof."

After an interval, the next report is:-

"That Mary Brown of Slowly has been brought to bed of a male
bastard child on the fourth of June last past and that John Smith
of Surely is the father of the said child."

The upshot is that he is convicted, signs the Bastardy Bond
and pays up, possibly after a period in prison awaiting trial.

**g.** Run for it and join the Army or Navy. Service in the Royal forces
was a bar against prosecution. If the process had already started,
the date and place of enlistment and the name of the man's officer
and regiment will be entered in the Assize roll.  The latter records are mostly at the county record offices as Quarter Sessions
records, and some have been printed or indexed in annual sections.

Even when a man had signed the Bond or been convicted, the parish
still had to get the money from him.  If he was poor, but had a
father who was well-to-do, then the father might be asked to counter-
sign the Bond and guarantee payment. If there were no rich relations,
the man's parish would be asked to pay.  This might not be where he
happened to be living at the moment, but was his parish of settlement, from which he could claim support in time of trouble.  Another
series of forms will cover the attempt of the girl's parish to discover the man's legal parish and get money from them.  There were
twenty possible forms printed to cope with all the ins and outs of
bastardy and another dozen for settlement questions.  All of these
would have been in the parish chest.

Another document which may assist is an Apprenticeship indenture –
possibly among other parish chest papers, if the child was a parish
(poor) apprentice, but probably now at the county record office.
Some natural fathers took an interest – especially if the child was
a boy – and paid for his apprenticeship to a good trade.  A counter-
signature on the indenture, for no apparent reason, may be a clue to
parentage, though it is not evidence enough by itself.

## Nonconformists

The entries of baptisms in chapel registers rarely show the name
of the father of a bastard, probably because immoral behaviour was
regarded more strictly, and the registers were far more open to in-
spection than church ones then, so no (male) clerk wanted to brand
a male member of the flock with such a charge, for all to see. There
is generally some comment in the minute books of the chapel, since
the girl (and, rarely, the man too) would be called before the elders
and made to confess to her terrible wickedness.   These minute books
may be at the chapel, or deposited in the CRO. Very few exist before
1800, and those that do have sometimes been printed, as rarities.

Before 1837, there were some hardy chapel folk who refused to go
to church even for weddings.   Before 1754, an ordained priest could
marry them. Some of the chapel pastors had been ordained in the past,
and seen the error of their ways, so they could and did marry their
flock.   After 1754, only marriage by a beneficed clergyman in a
licensed church (normally the parish church) was legal, except for
Quakers and Jews, whose records were much better than the average
church's.  Some other nonconformists continued to marry before their
own pastors, and fewer of these were ex-Church of England clergy or
even from the minor orders of clergy.   These marriages were illegal
and the children illegitimate, except in the eye of God.   Unfortun-
ately, it wasn't the Anglican God from whom all blessings flowed,
including personal property, so when it came to inheritance of the
father's estate, neither "wife" nor children were entitled to take
it.   This meant either that the father had to make an exceedingly
watertight will, leaving his estate to his "wife" as "Mary Jones now
known as Mary Robinson by repute" and branding his children as bastards, or that they had to find a church which would marry them without forcing them to be baptised first.   The latter course was safer
where real estate was concerned, since a brother who did not share
the man's religious principles might challenge the children's inheritance of it.  A great deal of property was entailed to "my son X and
his heirs lawful for ever", and the offspring of these pastor-married
unions were not lawful within the meaning of the act.

Most counties had several "places of resort" where the clergyman
of a small parish was happy to turn an honest penny by marrying anyone to anyone, if his palm was crossed with silver. Most got in job
lots of marriage licences, which the intending couple could buy and
marry on the spot.   This got over the need to have banns called in
the local parish church and thus give time for pressure towards bap-
tism to mount.

Obviously, if a family had no property (or real estate) at all,
they might risk a chapel "marriage", but the poorer they were, the
more likely they were to need parish relief, and this was heavily
geared to conventional (and church going) families.   Children born
as "bastards" could be sent back to the parish of their birth for
support, which could split a family up.   On the whole, most chapels
agreed to let their members marry according to the law, after 1754.

## Alias names in parish registers

Often you will find a family surname expressed as "Smith alias
(or als) Jones". Obviously, the most common reason for this is illegitimacy, normally where the father has publicly acknowledged the
child as his. It also occurs in nonconformist families where there
has been only a chapel wedding. The person/s involved and the legitimate descendants may use one name at one time and the other, or
the complete alias, at others. He can settle on one after a few years,
or on moving to a new parish where the double version is unknown.

There are other reasons for an alias name, for a legitimate child.
A young child brought up by a stepfather, grandparents or an uncle
will tend to be known by the name of the head of the household, and
may have some trouble reverting to his own. An apprentice or long
term employee might be known by the name of his master or of the
place where he worked. The second surname might be taken as an adult
under the terms of a will, in particular by the son in law or grand-
son of a man with no male heir of his own. It could be a simple
spelling variant (Messenger alias Massingberd) or represent indecision
between a locative and an occupational surname (Hathaway alias Gar-
dener). People who come in with a foreign surname are very likely
to have it altered to fit local tongues (Lefebure alias Feaver,
Teinturier alias Dyer). Some of these occur very early. Families
of Welsh descent on the borders may dither between keeping the
father's surname and altering it to a patronymic.

## Victorian attitudes

Under the new Poor Law of 1834, the poor were no longer the sole
responsibility of their parish of settlement, but collectively of
their "Union" of a group of parishes. "Out-relief" - paying allow-
ances to paupers in their own homes, and the rent if necessary - was
largely ended and the poor were shovelled into the Union workhouse,
which might be miles from home. Workhouse masters were often cruel
and grasping. Strangers and pregnant girls, like the aged, sick and
widows, were bullied and made to feel ashamed of poverty. Unless
their families could or would help, the workhouse it had to be - and
a baby who survived that sort of beginning was tough. Not all workhouse records are complete or survive at all, but if so, they are
likely to be at the county record office or large town library.

The father of the child might be taken to court, at the Petty
Sessions, and the case reported in lurid detail in the local papers.
As time wore on, surface morality made this publicity something which
those who could do so would pay anything to avoid. The tougher men
would horsewhip editors who offended too, which meant that by the
end of the century, only cases involving poor persons were reported
and only if they had "interesting" details. This century, such
"domestic" cases tend not to be reported normally, until recent years,
and now the trend is to mention cases concerning the rich and famous
only.

The most important commandment in Victorian times was "Thou shalt not be Found Out". The manoeuvres which the upper classes had always used to conceal an indiscretion now spread to the middle and lower middle classes. Those who could afford it went abroad or far from home. Mother might pad herself up to simulate pregnancy and take over her daughter's child, which was plausible enough for the eldest but sometimes carried to ridiculous lengths to cover for a younger daughter. The locals might be suspicious, but the child might believe Granny was Mother until he was adult. Frequently, the truth might not be told till the child married (or at all), or on the mother's deathbed. But sometimes the revelation was forced because a romantic attachment grew between those who had a parent in common.

Victorians had a number of euphemisms for illegitimacy to avoid saying the dreadful word bastard.

Natural child - in former times you will find a child described in a will as "natural" if he is the own child of a testator, not a stepchild. The legal expression, "natural and lawful", was just the usual repetition, but Victorians seemed to think it was an alternative (a "natural" also meant an idiot in their terms).

Other terms for the child are: left-hand; chance child; come-by-chance; misbegotten; love-child; mistake; bye-blow; slip; incubus; on the wrong side of the blanket; sinister.

The mother was: in trouble; up the stick or the spout; in a certain condition; fallen; slipped; tripped; unfortunate; lost; broken-kneed/winged/or legged; ruined; had strayed or sinned.

In this sort of climate, the revelation that a girl was going to have a baby "without a father" produced shock waves. Small wonder that she would often delay telling the family until it was too late to consider abortion by taking a herbal draught, which had been used by some in earlier days, though the dangers and unreliability of the method deterred most girls.

The only palliative was rapid marriage, to the father or anyone who offered, however unsuitable, and a carefully staged "premature" birth. Where the family had any local pretensions, even small ones, the girl would otherwise be sent away, thrown out entirely or encouraged to find a home elsewhere, possibly with a lowly relative, masquerading as a widow.

In London, it was possible to find anonymity, and perhaps a mechanical abortion. Given a little money, a place in one of the lodging houses or charity Homes for Fallen Women could be found. The private houses were often spotting grounds for likely prostitutes, so the innocent girl who had once been seduced might have no chance to get back on the straight and narrow. The old song "She was Poor but she was Honest" is a very fair summing up of the likely career of a village girl who "lost her honest name" and went to London.

## Official records

A standard birth certificate after 1837 for a bastard normally shows the mother's name and occupation, with a blank where the father's name should be. If the father actually went along with the mother and signed the notification, then his name would be entered too - but not if she gave it alone. A married woman's name is written as "Mary Smith formerly Jones", but the mother on this sort of certificate is given her maiden name alone, "Mary Jones". The legal surname would be that of the mother, but if the couple later married, the father's name might be consistently used as an adult. If you find an ancestor with no birth registration, try the mother's maiden name (from the birth certificate of a younger sibling) and see if the ancestor was registered as that.

A determined couple could pretend to be married when they were not, and register the children as legitimate. In the country, someone would probably let the official know, sooner or later, but in a town, especially in London, no one knew or cared, unless the children tried to claim an inheritance, and had to show the non-existent marriage certificate.

Occasionally, one or both of the couple changed names to avoid detection by the legal spouse or the police. This is difficult, though sometimes the disguise is a transparent one, like reversing their surnames, or using his mother's surname. Even when a new name was chosen, it might have some link with the old home and often the initials were retained.

Census records should be consulted for all persons alive before 1881. Some people lied to their children, but not the enumerator - in the country, he probably knew the truth anyway. Where the mother married after the birth of her child, you will want to know if the new husband is the natural father or not. The census entry may refer to the child as "son", or "son-in-law" (stepson) or "wife's son", which settles the matter. In 1841, no relationships are stated, but the stepchild will retain the old name in this document usually, and may be put out of sequence at the end of the family. A kindly man may treat him in every way as a son, which confuses the issue rather.

If you can locate the family in 1891 or 1901, it is possible to buy limited information from those censuses, but this will be age and birthplace, not the relationship to the head of household, and the cost is about £20, so it is not worth doing often.

If you can locate the child as an infant in an earlier census, it is worth noting down men with the same Christian name (and certainly any with his middle surname, if this is given). For a girl, there is less Christian name evidence, though sometimes the father's mother will have taken an interest - or the baby's mother will have had the nerve to use her name for this "left hand" grandchild.

After 1881, there are a few other official records which help. If you know where the girl was nine months before the baby's birth, find out who was in the house, from electoral rolls or rating records, or street directories. Try to trace the actual house where the baby was born too, and try to assess its size - mother may have been a servant there or a lodger, and the owner is not necessarily the culprit, but can be checked on.

Electoral rolls should be at the town or county record office. They will include owners of property and major tenants only until 1914, when all adult males are listed, regardless of status. Females are not listed until 1918 and only those over 30 until 1928. From then onwards, the rolls are good evidence of cohabitation in the simple sense.

## Legitimation

If the parents of a bastard child married subsequently, he was by custom regarded as a legitimate child and assumed his father's name, although sometimes special provision had to be made for him to inherit property which was devised to "heirs lawful of the body" of so and so. He could not inherit a title, however. Sometimes the eldest sons of peers who had married too late contested this point - especially if there had been a fake marriage to seduce the mother initially - and the case was fully reported by the House of Lords. The "secret marriage" at an earlier date would be claimed but not proven and the younger brothers would inherit. Occasionally there had been a genuine marriage abroad, but if it wasn't performed by an Anglican clergyman and reported back, it didn't count. Most couples who married abroad did marry again in England, if they had any property to leave.

By an Act of 1926, it was legally permitted that, provided the couple had been free to marry when the child was born, he or she became legitimate on subsequent marriage. The children had to be re-registered and the only giveaway is the long gap between date of birth and date of registration. If you know such a marriage took place, it is worth checking for later registration. A lot of children of "Deceased Wife's Sister" marriages were legitimated in this way. It still didn't work for inheritance of titles.

From 1959, children can be legitimated by a subsequent marriage even if the parent/s were married to someone else at the time. Children of incest cannot be legitimated ever.

## Adoptions

The taking over of responsibility for another man's child by a stepfather, grandfather, uncle, employer or other person was formerly done without formality. Stepchildren were mostly assimilated into the family and even took the stepfather's name, as well as, or instead of, their own. Grandparents or married sisters might bring up the children of an unmarried girl as their own. Masters, especially childless ones, adopted promising apprentices and academics bright children from the lower classes. A few men even adopted female children to train them up as suitable future wives. Except for the last class, the adoption probably worked out to the advantage of the child.

In 1926, there was legislation to control adoption. The adopter had to be 21 years older than the adoptee (or 30 years for a child of the opposite sex) and the adoption was supposed to be registered and entered on the Adopted Children's Register. Even after this, there were still a lot of privately arranged adoptions, via doctors, solicitors and churches, as there had been during the 1914-18 War, when a War baby boom coincided with rising infertility among the upper and middle classes. The best men went to war and were killed or came back gassed - which produced sterility. Adoption Societies, mostly run by religious bodies, arranged the transfer of children of the poor to the childless rich and were intent on obliterating all traces of the natural parents, who might turn up and embarrass the adopters.

The Adoption Certificate gives the date of birth correctly, but only the names of the adopting parents appear, not the natural ones. Even if the mother is the natural mother of the child, the certificate does not say so. The idea is to sever all links with the past and make the child a full legal member of the new family. This is fine until you want to trace your own ancestors.

By the Act of 1974, persons over 18 were for the first time permitted access to information about their original birth. There are very strict controls over this, for obvious reasons. An adoptee must first write to The General Register Office (CA Section), Box 7, Titchfield, Fareham, Hants. PO15 5RU for an application form (don't send details at this stage). The form asks for the details from the Adoption Certificate (from St. Catherine's House) of your present name, surname, adoptive parents and date of adoption, plus which country you were born in and at which court you were adopted, if you know.

The next stage is an obligatory session with a Counsellor, at St. Catherine's, the local Social Security Office or the one in the adoption area. He will explain the process and the pitfalls, and if you still want to go ahead, will then give you details of your original name, your mother's name, your father's name if it is on your birth certificate, and the name of the Court where the adoption took place, plus an authorisation for the court to give you further details if it has any. You can then buy your original birth certificate from St. Catherine's (£5.00) on which will be the exact place of birth and the father's (or mother's) occupation and the name of the notifier, usually the mother.

A legitimate child might have been adopted because he/she was an orphan; because the mother was left a poor widow; because the father deserted his family; because a widowed or divorced mother remarried; because the parents were inadequate, feckless, criminal, cruel or plain bad in every way. The court record will probably tell you, if you are mature enough to take it. Some courts destroy old records, or they are incomplete, especially where the adoption was through a private person or agency. You can perfectly well trace back from the birth certificate in the normal way without trying to contact your natural parents, which is something you might regret.

If you were illegitimate, the father's name may appear, if there
was stable cohabitation, in which case, you may be able to proceed.
If not, the court record might give the information.   Some courts
have lost the papers or never had a complete record anyway.   They
could give you the name of any private adoption society, the local
authority or solicitor involved in the matter, but here again, the
records may be missing, unless the adoption was in the last twenty
years.   Solicitors and doctors can be very sticky indeed about re-
vealing details.   Batter away, if you think there is information,
but don't get hysterical, or they will never tell you.

If these official sources don't work, you will have to ask your
adoptive parents, who may not know, or may get very upset that you
are rejecting them after all they have done for you.   Or you could
try tracing your mother.   She may have married (work through St.
Catherine's indexes) and be readily findable under her new name.
But be careful.   She will not necessarily welcome the arrival on her
doorstep of a total stranger saying "Hello Mum".   If this episode in
her life is safely buried, it may cause undue pain and worry to re-
surrect it.   Write and arrange to see her elsewhere, if she will.
Better still, phone and don't leave a detailed message with someone
else.   Remember you are unlikely to feel instant rapport with a
stranger, who just happens to have given birth to you umpteen years
before.   You may hate her on sight and be sorry you ever gave the
dreadful creature your address.   The same applies with greater force
to your illegitimate father.   A deserted woman may have very good
reasons, connected with the child's welfare, for giving it for adoption - but what was his excuse?

Some mothers have written to Counsellors asking to be put in touch
with their lost children if they apply.   A few have said they reject
the idea utterly. Getting in touch is never a thing to be undertaken
lightly, on either side.

If you can trace a parent up to a certain period, then the trail
goes cold, you could write a letter, enclosed in another to Special
Section, Room 101b. Dept. of Health and Social Security, Records
Branch, Newcastle upon Tyne NE98 1YU.   You will need to give the cur-
rent name of the person, date of birth or rough age, last known
address and any other details, like last known employer, which will
enable them to trace him/her.   They won't give you the address, but
will forward the letter, which the parent can answer if inclined.

You may get information from old residents who remember your
mother where you were born, if not too far back; you may be able to
trace an aunt or grandmother who will talk more freely than your
mother will.   Workmates or boozing pals may be bribed into talking
about your father - but be careful.   You could lay yourself open to
scroungers willing to say anything to please you, as long as you are
paying.   But retired milkmen may know a lot.

The Counsellors try to warn you against pursuing the hunt, if you
are young and vulnerable.   Don't ignore them because you are sure
*your* background, *your* parents, will be wonderful and romantic.   It

is far more likely to be trashy, grubby and commonplace.  If you
discover the truth, try to understand, and don't judge too harshly
or let it cloud the present.

## Family traditions

Very often, it was not much of a secret who the father of a bastard was.  The child would be told as an adult, at marriage, at the
mother's deathbed.  Or, if a possible romantic association with a
half-brother or sister seemed likely.  Incest overcame prudery.
However, sometimes family traditions are downright lies, or wishful
thinking.

Even the most prudish of Victorian aunts would accept the awful
shame of illegitimacy as long as the father was a gentleman - the
local squire, or, preferably, a member of the Royal family.  This
encouraged a scared girl to name the wrong man and for families to
fake such a descent many years later.  The number of children that
George III is supposed to have had by Hannah Lightfoot would be
difficult to fit into that Quaker girl's brief life, apart from her
respectable though non-Quaker marriage to Isaac Axford.  A lot of
bastards claimed Royal descent after reading the pamphlets of
"Princess Olive of Cumberland" (Mrs Serres), a brilliant forger and
romantic genealogist.  If the family tradition comes only from an
aunt with a weakness for romantic novels, forget it.

Even when the tradition is old, inspect it carefully.  Is the
suggested father old enough?  Did he live in the same place, or come
into contact with the girl at the right time?  If Granny was a maid
at the Manor, she might well have fallen a victim to the wicked
Squire or his son - but equally, the butler, or the bootboy or the
gamekeeper might have done it.  Try to compare a photograph of the
child with portraits of the rest of the nominal family and with the
Squire's family.  If he looks quite unlike the one and very like the
other, then this is corroboration but not proof.  He might hark back
to an earlier ancestor (who might, of course, really be a bastard
of an earlier Squire).

If a rich man dun it, there was generally a pay-off.  If the
mother was set up in a shop or bought a husband, if the child re-
ceived a mystery gift to apprentice him, if there was sudden improve-
ment in the financial status of a girl from a poor family, someone
with money is likely to have been involved - rarely just out of
charitable impulse.  If you have a name, check the man's will - a
surprising number of pre-Victorian men conscientiously looked after
their bastards.  Even some later wills are frank about "my baseborn
son" or leave sums to "the boy known as William Harris" or to "William son of Mary wife of John Green".  This could be sheer benevo-
lence, but this usually expresses itself in general charitable be-
quests, not legacies to one child of one woman.  Some men left money
on trust, through a solicitor, or felt they had done enough with the
initial payment.

Collections of gentry family diaries, either published or deposited in the record office, are worth combing for indiscreet references at the time. Spinster relatives sometimes took an interest in pretty bastards of the men of the family, from religious duty. Old records deposited by solicitors may reveal mystery payments which cover attempts at blackmail or conscience money.

If the presumed father was "in society", it is practically certain that any scandal about him will figure in the published diaries or correspondence of known gossips - like Pepys, Evelyn, Horace Walpole or Creevey (himself the bastard of Lord Sefton). A chatty book of reminiscences may give the game away about friends. Negative evidence, that a putative father was exploring the Zambesi for the whole year concerned, is as useful in settling matters.

## "If I had my rights..."

Even if you can prove to your own satisfaction that Grandpa was the illegitimate son of a Duke, you cannot go off and claim the title. Bastardy is an absolute bar to that. The Victorians called it the "bar sinister", after the practice of granting the coat of arms with, sometimes, a diagonal bend (not a bar) to a promising bastard of a peer. You cannot use a coat or arms like this unless the College of Arms grants it, at vast expense.

If a rich man left his estate to "all my children", in the past a bastard son could not claim a share. Legally, he did not exist. Children are by definition legitimate children. A man wishing to leave money or property to a bastard had better use one of the phrases like "my baseborn son"; "the child known as William Brown"; "my children which I had by Elizabeth Harris spinster, known as Tom, Dick and Harry Harris or Jones".

If a bastard was left property under a will, but for some reason did not claim it, his legitimate descendents might be able to under certain circumstances, provided time had not run out under the Statute of Limitations. If he died before the testator, the legacy would have lapsed anyway. The bastard could inherit from his mother, if there were no legitimate children, but not through her from a grandparent, unless he were specifically named.

A mistress and children, however lavishly supported in the man's lifetime, had no claim at all after his death, unless he had already made provision by a settlement or trust. If it was a secret trust, whereby a friend was given money "for the purpose of which he knows", the friend could default without redress, unless a signed contract promised payment.

Since 1969, illegitimate children do have the right to claim maintenance from the father's estate on the same basis as legitimate ones. It is necessary to prove paternity, though, which might not be easy. Going to law is expensive and might wipe out any gain from the estate. "All my children" now means bastards as well and the intestacy rules apply equally too (see *Somerset House Wills* in this series). Illegitimate children can still be ruled out of a share in the will of any relative except the father or mother, unless they are minors, handicapped or in great want (and have a very good lawyer).

Legitimated children (see page 12) can claim under a will or clause which comes into operation after they are legitimated or anyway from 1969. Adopted children belong to the adoptive family, not the natural one, so cannot claim from the natural father's estate even if they are legitimate children.

Basically, forget about making money from finding your real parents/grandparents. Let knowledge be its own reward.

## Scotland

The situation in Scotland is similar to that for nonconformists. They were far stricter about illicit sex officially, and although arrangements for the poor were slightly different, moral pressure ensured that the parish wanted full details about who did what with whom amang the heather. The "examinations" are recorded in the Kirk Sessions Books, a sort of parish minute book deposited with the registers at New Register House, Edinburgh. The guilty parties had to sit on the stool of repentence before the assembled congregation for a number of Sundays, according to the gravity of the offence.

However, in the nineteenth century, the system of housing male farm servants and even females in bothies or chambers separate from the farm house gave licence rein, and illegitimacy soared. Female farm labourers managed because they could have their children with them – domestics lost their place with their honour.

The situation was complicated by the custom of "handfast marriage". If a couple stated before two witnesses that they intended to marry, and took hands on it, they were married with the force of law, for all purposes except inheritance of titles and some property. These irregular marriages may never have been recorded, yet be perfectly legal. Later there was provision for registration with the sheriff clerk. The marriage was not legal in England, so couples crossing the border had better marry formally. The custom is still in force, and any couple living together are regarded as married "by habit and repute". The custom extended to England much later as a "common law marriage" – which isn't legal but gives claim to maintenance by court order.

There were a great many problems with regard to succession to property and old peerage titles of Scottish nobility (peerages of the United Kingdom could be claimed by clearly legitimate heirs only) and only the very determined got anywhere with claims to these from a handfast marriage. But for ordinary purposes, the children are not bastards at all. Obviously, there could not be a handfast marriage while one of the parties had a lawful spouse alive.

## A Bastardy Bond

*Edited transcript of the facsimile handwritten original opposite, reproduced by kind permission of the P.C.C. of Wendover from a document now deposited in the County Record Office.   Printed forms were later available for the purpose.*

Know All Men by these presents that We William Playstow Junr. Son of William Playstow Senr. of Lee Als. Lea in the County of Bucks. Gentleman And Richard Dell of Wendover in the sd. County of Bucks. Collermaker Are held and Firmly bound Unto Thomas Benning of Wendover Yeoman and Joseph Parnam of Wendover Yeoman Churchwardens of the parish of Wendover and Robert Kipping of Wendover Gentleman William Picton of Wendover Carpenter and William Collet of Wendover Gentleman Overseers of the poor of the parish of Wendover in the sum of Fourty pounds of Lawfull Money of Great Britaine To be paid to the said Thomas Benning Joseph Parnam Robert Kipping William Pickton and William Collet their Successors Attorneys Executors Administrators or Assigns To Which payment well and truely to be made We bind us and both of us by himself for the whole and in the whole Our and both of Our Heirs Executors and Administrators Firmly by these presents Sealed with our Seals dated the Twentysixth day of April in the sixth Year of the Reigne of our Sovraigne Lord George the Second by the Grace of God of Great Britaine France and Ireland King Defender of the Faith &c In the Year of our Lord God 1733.

The Condition of this Obligation is Such That Whereas Mary Wesson of the parish of Wendover Single Woman (daughter of Joseph Wesson of Wendover Butcher) hath of Late been delivered of a female Bastard Child within the parish of Wendover and hath made Oath before Two of his Majestys Justices of the peace for this County that the within Bounden William Playstow Junr. is the Father of the said Bastard Child, If therefore the said William Playstow and the above bound Richard Dell or either of them do and shall from time to time and at all times fully and clearly acquitt and discharge Save harmless and Indemnifie as well the above named Church Wardens and overseers of the poor their successors for the time being as also the Inhabitants and parishioners of the parish of Wendover from all Manner of Expences Costs and Charges which shall at any time hereafter Arise happen by reason of the Birth Maintenance Education and Bringing up of the said Bastard child ...

|  |  |
|---|---|
| John Senior | Will. Plaistowe Jun. |
| Richd. Bigg | Richard Dell |

Know all Men by these presents That We William Playstowe Jun, Son of William Playstowe ... of ... Als ... in the County of Bucks Gentleman, And Richard Doll of Wendover in the said County of Bucks Collarmaker Are held and firmly bound unto Thomas Bowning of Wendover aforesaid in the said County of Bucks Yeoman and Joseph Farnum of the parish of Wendover aforesaid Yeoman Churchwardens of the parish of Wendover aforesaid And Robert Kipping of Wendover aforesaid Gentleman, William Stichton of Wendover aforesaid Carpenter and William Collet of the parish of Wendover aforesaid Gentleman, Overseers of the poor of the parish of Wendover aforesaid in the Sum of Fourty pounds of Lawfull Money of Great Brittaine To be paid to the said Thomas Bowning Joseph Farnum Robert Kipping William Stichton and William Collet their Successors Executors Administrators or Assigns To which payment well and truly to be made we and both of us by himself for the whole and in the whole bind ourselves and both of us Our Heirs Executors and Administrators firmly by these presents Sealed with our Seals Dated the Twenty Sixth day of April in the Sixth year of the Reigne of our Soveraigne Lord George the Second by the Grace of God Great Brittaine ffrance and Ireland King Defender of the ffaith &c In the year of our Lord God 1736

The Condition of this Obligation is Such That whereas one Mary Watson of the parish of Wendover being a Woman Daughter of Joseph Watson of the parish of Wendover aforesaid Instructed hath of Late been delivered of a female Bastard Child within the parish of Wendover within written And whereas it hath been made Oath before Two of his Majesty's Justices of the peace for this County that the within named William Playstowe Jun is the ffather of the said Bastard Child If therefore the said William Playstowe and Richard Doll or Either of them, their or Either of their Heirs Executors or Administrators do and shall from time to time and at all times hereafter ... save harmless and Indemnified as well the above named Thomas Bowning Joseph Farnum Robert Kipping William Stichton and William Collet Churchwardens and overseers of the poor of the parish of Wendover aforesaid and their Successors for the time being and every of them As also all the Inhabitants ... parishioners of the said parish of Wendover aforesaid Which now are or hereafter shall be for the time being and every of them of and from all and all Manner of Expences Costs and Charges whatsoever which shall or may at any time hereafter Arise happen come grow or be Imposed upon them or Either or ... of them for or by reason or means of the Birth Maintenance Education and Bringing up of the said Bastard Child and of and from all Actions Suits Troubles Damages and Demands whatsoever touching or concerning the same Then this Obligation shall be void and of none Effect or Else shall Stand remaine and be in full force ... power and Vertue

Sealed and Delivered in the presence of being first duly Stamped

John Senior
Richd Rigg

Will Playstowe Jun
Richard Doll

## An Examination Concerning Bastardy

*Transcript of the facsimile original opposite, reproduced by kind permission of the P.C.C. of Wendover from a document now deposited in the County Record Office.*

Bucks. The Examination of Anne Swift of Wendover in ye County of Bucks. aforesaid Single woman Taken upon Oath before us Fra. Ligo & Rich. Saunders Esqrs. two of his Majestys Justices of ye Peace of & for ye said County this third day of Janry. Anno Dm 1732.

*     *     *     *     *     *     *     *     *     *     *     *     *     *     *     *     *     *     *     *

This Examinant being duely sworn and Examin'd saith & deposeth That She this Examt. having Contracted an acquaintance with one Tobias Brooks of Princes Risboro' in ye said County Laceman He ye said Tobias Brooks by his importunities p$^{re}$vailed upon her this Examt. Sometime about Christmas which was in ye year 1731 or in ye Holly–days to have Carnall knowledge of ye body of her this Examt. which he then had & has frequently since had 'till about six weeks before Mich$^{mus}$ last & that as often as any oppertunity offerr'd this examt. during all that time living at Princes Risboro' aforesaid very near to ye dwelling house of Thomas Brooks father of ye said Tobias with whom ye said Tobias then dwelt And this Examt. further saith that at sometime during such her familiarity with ye said Tobias Brooks & at his having Carnall knowledge of her body as aforesaid he ye said Tobias Brooks begott her this Examt. with Child of a female Bastard Child of which she has been since deliver'd at Wendover aforesaid (vizt) on ye 26th day of October last which said female child is now living And this Examt. further saith that no other person whatsoever ever had carnall knowledge of her body before she was deliver'd of such female child.

The mark of

Jur. apud Aylesbury in Com. p$^{rd}$to                    Anne  X  Swift
Coram Nobis, Fra. Ligo, R. Saunders.

This is a true Coppy examin'd
this 8th day of Jan$^{ry}$· 1732. By me;
Deverell Dagnall.